The Moonmen

The Moonmen

Anna Livesey

Victoria University Press

TE WHARE WĀNANGA O TE ŪPOKO O TE IKA A MĀUI

VICTORIA
UNIVERSITY OF WELLINGTON

VICTORIA UNIVERSITY PRESS
Victoria University of Wellington
PO Box 600 Wellington
www.victoria.ac.nz/vup

National Library of New Zealand Cataloguing-in-Publication Data

Livesey, Anna, 1979-
The moonmen / Anna Livesey.
Poems.
ISBN 978-0-86473-626-0
1. New Zealand poetry—21st century. 1. Title.
NZ821.3—dc 22

Published with the support of a grant from

ARTS COUNCIL OF NEW ZEALAND *TOI AOTEAROA*

Printed by Printlink, Wellington

Poem on Efficiency

What debonair efficiency
to unicycle to university!

Contents

I The Moonmen

II Midwestern

III Mother

for Hamish

I The Moonmen

Young Love

Your body held the awkwardness of a breaking voice—
the obvious metaphor holds true, a young animal, clumsy,
still surprised by itself.

★

Remember a night in a tent on the south coast?
A cautious night, a play at touching.

★

In the last flush of summer we spent all our pocket money,
ate lunch in the olive grove, kissed in the grass.

Your father died, my mother got sick.

We slept in a blue room under the garage.
Days tumbled after one another.
Families opened and shut in new shapes.
I wrote poems in praise of your body.

★

February, the Eastbourne sun.
The world gathered to watch us break a glass,
hold a bunch of flowers, kiss.
This was the year of making a display, of moving north.

★

In our first flat we lived on the edge of a gully,
under the hospital's constant mistresses,
the swarming helicopters and the ambulances,
crying out their needs as they rode up to the door.

It was quiet in that big city—
you and I in the roiling nest of a million people,
you and I, and the others, passing around us.

★

On Grafton Bridge I met a suicide.
We talked, I held her arm.
'Not again, Lois,' said the policewoman,
her impatient blood jingling through her veins.

★

The window glass in our favourite cafe sent our faces back
        to us, distorted.
We loved them, and they were far away.
We had been away. We came back.

★

What is the half-life of a dying brain?
What government will compensate the survivors?

★

The wooden floors of our second flat glowed a perfect,
    delicious gold.
In the eye of the night we made love.
We befriended a cat.
There were things to be getting on with, if not quite
the things we'd had in mind.

Bone Collecting
—*for Biddy*

Weasel skull, or little cat, animal wild
or tame, makes no difference now. Chambers open, dry
where the soft channels kept movement, whatever version
of pleasure, noise, contusion, pain.

★

River bend. Bones water-dropped, hunted
among the clay and stones—clavicle, rib, also
knucklebones, knocking in the hand.
Rattled in a saucepan until—clean, white,
still chalkily warm—they scatter between us, shards and
      patterns
on the flowered carpet.

★

Grafted pear tree, three fruit shapes and subtle tastes.
The speckled pears come last of all.
Hands searching windfalls turn up a tusk.
Earth-yellowed, splintered, mitred to a cutting edge,
it rose to your fingers—pointed evidence,
the last wild boar of Kelburn.

Ice-Pickles

Elision and the small cuts made without reference to light, movement. You are walking, stepping quietly. I am behind you, aristocratic hunter, turn-tailed fox, the colour of your hair lightening, sun taking off from the trees. It is November, things are beginning to grow—the terraced garden takes sun on its long flank, leaves turn this way and that, there is the smell of daffodils. The cupboards, as always, need cleaning. There is a small child, saying something no doubt adorable. What turns we take on this, me walking behind, yesterday in front. It is the season after winter—what rain there was then, what splendid ice-pickles.

Dear Geordie

I'm not sure how old we were—nine or ten I suppose,
old enough that I was aware of you
as we walked across the paddocks under the thousands
        of stars.

The eels swarm in the creek where it enters the bush—
dark and gurgling steadily, banks slippery with tree
        roots and litter,
the smell that rises off the water,
deep rich rot and the pepper of crushed leaves.

You handed the torch over.
Crouched on black roots, you tipped the possum out of
        the bag,
turned its curled body belly-up and sliced,
'so the eels can smell the guts'.

Night and the smell of bush. The things I thought about
        your body.
The beam of light from my hand on the pale fur,
unseaming redly under your blade.

The Mousing Song of the Grandfather

One way bridge, always the sign
of near arrival. Ditch, willow tree,
memory of departure. World ship-sewn,
never reversed. Those first months,
nothing more than difficulty—save that one day
at Eastbourne—wind, your hair, the baby
asleep among the seagrass.
I lay on the blanket and smoked.
Now things are moving on—it is evening,
not yet five and already you are falling asleep.
I cannot wonder at it. I can recall
picture and environment, paths between the trees.
I can call the dogs we had, in order—Sire, Callie,
Lucy, Patch. The white cat who never earned her keep.
All those days I came home, walking up over the creek.

Perrymead

There was no garden or bush, only bare grass and a house, very close on the left. A new house, built to look old. Written in stone letters above the door was the word 'Community'. There were several other houses nearby in what used to be the piggery. The creek had disappeared and the hills were much, much flatter.

Report from the Front

Very dark, quiet. Anxious ground birds scutter, I would if I could. Some nights I wake and all I can think of is clematis, the wild vine you found out beyond the back paddock. How are little Kitty and Eva and Maude? The funny thing is, there is always mist here, and movement—and some days the boys say they smell things, you know.

Homesicknessness

Little seat above the big blue harbour,
grass long enough to fold above us, seed-heads
and nasturtiums, orange trumpets over leaves,
round and lifted on the air.

Long Time Watching

The tiny heart flutters,
too inward, too circumspect.
What body turns against itself?
What hope expels its only wish?

The pink and blue dresses flow and flutter.
The little girls lever the swings,
their whole fierce bodies
driving them up.

Gravity, less easily fooled, holds the two of you.
Your hands flutter against each other.
Your legs and backs press
into the wooden slats of the bench.

In a curve above the earth built of her own power
your only daughter swings
. . .
you spend a long time watching.

Fetish

I think of it
as your true guardian.

When you cry in the night
I tend you
because it never sleeps.

When I feed you
spoon by spoon
the mushed silverbeet,
the banana,
the porridge
and so on,

I feel its eyes on my back,
its thoughts bent towards me.

Be thankful it loves you.

Chrysalis
—for Steve Kramp

A difficult thing to hold,
a gold-fastened casket,
green and cold.

Open the door. Unfold
a chrysalis. Woven out of place.
A difficult thing to hold.

Thin black veins. Wings tightly rolled
under membrane: translucent,
green and cold.

Pain, sharp, changing, old
moves like water—
difficult to hold.

An accident, a broken mould—
or is the back a river, its water
green and cold?

At the edges, fingers move, fold.
A steady gaze, a steady touch:
things difficult to hold.

Skin sealed, wings shuttered and controlled
rest the chrysalis a moment in your hand.
It is difficult,
green and cold.

Poem for a Geography Teacher

Esker—the word like 'whisper',
saying of itself that it is the silence
left after water rubbed under ice,
after the molecules' loose regard for each other,
their silky insinuation.

There is death in the world, you have noticed it;
sickness and worry travel close companions.
The ice moves slowly, plucking grit and rock,
cracking substrate, the pieces
picked up and dropped, picked up and dropped.

Arrival

(One)

You were anxious but resplendent
in a dress so blue the bees dive-bombed it.

(Two)

You came in late.
There were petals on your shoes.

You had been standing, you said,
under the most perfect tree.

Bonsense

—*for Heather Tone*

Grass kingdom,
higher than headwise, horsewise.
A tree looks down on you from the roadside.

Paddock peopled with tiny horses,
a stirrup, leg-up, leg over,
more tiny size, more
proliferation of tinyness.

Un-joy, a kind of blank seriousness.
It doesn't live among the horses.

You are a long way away, in a library.
You say, if your small library were a body,
poetry would be the head and torso,
fiction a limb, reference a limb.

From the chest of your books,
you enjoin belief
in outposts of miniature sense or nonsense,
or going further, antonym, *bonsense*—
the elaborate folly of the heart and brain,
built curlicued, baroque.

What bonsense is this, a tiny horse, a tiny library?
The great iced cake of relationships,
the ornamental pony of compassion,
the perennial shout (SHOUT) of shared exclamation.

The Idea of Ordinary

Baker and his wife, a young girl from Hungary,
setting out from the coast to find the source of the Nile.
Baker thinking, as they rode, then walked through swamp,
then swam, that his wife's yellow hair is a light,
striking out before them.

One day, crossing a river, they come upon a tribe
        'previously unknown'.
Already wet, Mrs Baker chooses this moment
to kneel by the water and wash her hair.

Baker thinks of his first wife, dead four years,
his children—the two girls at school, the youngest, his son,
boarding with an aunt in Sussex.

Mrs Baker takes the long rope of hair in her hands,
twists and squeezes. Baker closes his eyes.

When he opens them, a small boy
stands beside his wife, his black hands
following her fingers as they comb through her hair.

The Moonmen

On the last night the moonmen came.
We woke at an unaccustomed time and knelt by the window.
The moonmen pushed lines out in front of them,
they marked off their territories with orange markers.
The moonmen made a regular *thud thud* like a generator.
They walked in spaces we were used to seeing cordoned off.
It was a strange light the moonmen moved in—
a greeny glow they brought themselves, a glow that reflected
off their white suits and off the shiny visors curving stiffly
across the front of their heads.
We were leaving in the morning and so we said
'the moonmen need not concern us', and
'we will pack up the kitchen and say goodbye to the cat'.
Still, it was a funny thing they came at just that time—-
I thought perhaps they were acting something out for us
while we crouched below the windowsill
and our knees grew tired and stiff.

Good Night Hibiscus

Terrace, little outlier, where the sky sheets blue, purple, bats flit up, pinning it like a backdrop in a school hall. I told a story that went on forever and reached no end. You looked steadily out past the hibiscus, no particular vision, no specific need to think. That was some time ago, and since then, certain things have started to bother me. Nothing moves more quickly than air, shifting over the landmass, bringing subtle changes that are what we mean when we say 'weather'. Nothing is larger or more obsolete than the sea, green-gold somewhere under that smooth, sheeting sky, taking up little items like seaweed and plastic bags, broken-up pieces of net, and laying them in lacy fronds across the sand. Goodnight, I should have said, wrapping up the conversation. Goodnight bats, terrace, goodnight hibiscus, pink and red as you are.

Couchant

—for Hamish

Six-thirty on a stormy Friday,
Henry the cat paces my desk, catches my eye.

I have become the early riser I always wanted to be.
Some part of my body, turning a corner, met itself there.

★

The red chillies are drying in their pot on the bookshelf.
I am typing, you are sleeping, upstairs the baby is growing.

She is growing so that, these last weeks, when I call home,
her mother, holding her by the phone says, 'She hears you,
          she's smiling.'
★

We were pair of sillies,
playing a brilliant, slanting, sliding game.

Teenage desire so sure of itself–so rampant, so the answer
to all its own questions.

★

Sunday mornings we take a borrowed baby and sit in a
        cafe—
you're so good with her says Constantina,

as she places the crimson coffee cup just beyond baby-reach.
You drink it one-handed, handling her gently.

★

Curled, patient, the heart does slow duty at the gate.
Stone pillars, lilac, the smell of crushed mint.

We are a pair of lions, facing across a crest.
We are as helpless as babies.

II Midwestern

Espy

The first thing I saw
was the inside of my own head—I did not know
what darkness was, or how it felt.
After the unwrapping I became
connected to everything.
The world rushed up, cramming itself
inside my eye—but my eye
is a small thing, round like a sparrow's head,
slimy as a cut gherkin.
Light pecked at me.
Broken shapes and a series of flashes.

I Was Lonely Without Them

I waved goodbye
to all the days that passed—my hand rubbing the air,
the days passing off
like a trail of refugees.

All the days that passed
were unrecognisable.
They spent time doing things
the law did not allow.

All the days had clocks in them,
they had iron sides
like battleships, and holes
through which I pointed the guns.

All the days that passed
were orange. The smell of burning rubber
dawned with them. They were not opposed to revision
but there was always a certain wait.

Midwestern

Midwestern like an unlocked bike, like heat rising and dipping the fifteen degrees between 90 and 105, like a thunderstorm that rushes cold air across everything, that breaks the silence with cracks and gashes, with rumbles. Midwestern like brats, that's braats, that's bratwurst, a legacy of the northern peasants who brought their spiced ground meat, well mixed with fat and encased in sausage casing. Midwestern like porches, and even more, like porch swings, where the locals really do sit holding hands, drinking beer, watching fireflies and listening to cicadas scratch their legs against their bodies in a frenzy of sound-making. Midwestern like the man who offers you a ride home with your new porch furniture, and the man you meet on the bridge, who studies solar heating and tells you 'we're good people here'. Midwestern like the other man you see once or twice a week, his grey beard straggling down his chest and his voice a sing-song monotony of cursing and disapprobation directed at the skinny daughter who walks next to him, sucking on a sucker and pushing her stringy hair back from her face. Midwestern like corn, corn, corn, and hogs and barns—at least, the ones near the highways—that look like storybook illustrations, red and curve-roofed, full of imagined hay and good-fellowship. Midwestern like the question, called from porches and on the streets, from pickups and in the shops of downtown Iowa City: is it hot enough for ya? Is it hot enough? Is it hot?

Cat Poem

Little silky grey and brown cat under the fuchsia bush at the edge of the lawn. She flips her small body upwards, bats at the springy branches. The red and pink flowers move above her like throats.

In the late summer heat she is as well occupied as any of us, wriggling on her back down the sloping grass towards the apple tree.

Ballad of Two Writers Meeting

Oh he was a poet and she was a fiction
and they didn't know what to say.

Or she was a poet and he was a fiction
and the words got in the way.

After the Burn Failed to Go Off

Drizzle sat in clusters on grass beside the bonfire.
Connie smoked half a cigarette then turned the butt under
      the ashes with a spade.
I was a long way from home.

★

There was a sway to the grass that reminded me of the
      harbour.
Across the field, a tree split the shadow.
I couldn't guess its name.

★

Making a cutting sign with her hands, Connie called off
      the burn.
Inside there was apple cider. I was still
a long way from home.

Walking and Other Seasons

A hill, wheel-tracks to follow, dry grass
that stands above my knees. Creek ice loosening.
Winter breaking, the body turns to movement.

I walked long, my coat, black and white,
swishing at my calves. Streets and lanes,
apple trees and concrete.

What the mind turns over is like
the leaves that reappear after the melt. A few shapes
worn to ribs, caught against the sidewalk, stained there.

Returning, I found a lantern on the porch,
and a bird's nest inside it. The maker a small creature,
passing back and forth through the glass mouth.

Dear Love

Dear Love, I woke this morning
in the middle of the bed.

Outside, light made squares and brackets
on the unswept leaves.

I sat in the front room
and was very disappointed.

Go

I was weeded, undesigned,
I caught nothing but garter snakes.
A wastrel, whale-headed, I was racy, roving.
I was lacy and needy, sober and serious.
Owl-like and shrew-like, I was waiting for news.

Lydia

—after two paintings of her sister by Mary Cassatt

I.
She has just stirred in the sugar—
the tea is still moving
as she draws the spoon over the lip of the cup.

She is alone—or rather, she is acting the pose 'alone',
leaning back into the pillowed chair,
her smile, tucked in at the edges, giving away the joke,
her hands managing that little bit of business with the spoon.

II.
In the second painting the brush has moved more slowly.
Lydia's jacket is loose, as though the fabric
cannot bear to touch her body.

She is making blue lace and the dull blue
reaches up to her face under the wide-brimmed hat.
Behind her, magenta flowers line the path to the greenhouse.

Portrait After

He felt strangely nothing but a lack of vocation.
She caught a taxi south.

★

All along the streets he collected
implements of family—rice cookers and harvest baskets,
small nicks in doorways marking the heights of children.

★

At the edge of the inlet, she dabbled in water.
Behind the boatshed the driver rolled deft cigarettes.

Night

—*for Heather Tone*

Streetlight shows leaf-shapes
burned into the sidewalk.

The white tail of a rabbit
starts across a lawn.

A bridge and we cross it, creek
making dark water noise below.

Memory of a Poem by August Kleinzahler

A crowd and two people (one in a blue dress).
They stood outside the ring the crowd made
around some spectacle
and spoke to each other.
It is not in the poem, but I think she folded her hands
in the skirt of her blue dress,
running the fabric between her fingers.
I think he touched her wrist, bare and white
in the light reflected from the spectacle.
They were behind the backs of several thousand people,
none of whom noticed them. Her wrist
looked very fine as it rose from the blue material.
Seeing the wrist, he was sorry for what he had said.
He said something else to her instead and she replied, quietly.
They made a small crowd of their own.

Dear Alfred, I Have Been Meaning to Write

Dear Alfred, I have been meaning to write, but some small incidence has always held me back. Yesterday, a black feather—one among many, leaving the flock. Today, no reason, only the small procession locked in a drawer, marching jauntily, indifferent or unaware that nobody will watch them.

It came as a surprise to receive your letter. I thought after all this time you would have given up on stamps, but there it was, a portrait you licked and offered to me. Never in life, Alfred, have you seen things grow with the certain virtue they do here—the fleshy leaves of the bulbs present themselves with such insouciant zeal. Someday I must send you a snap: tips and strips all over, a bunch of blooming, a hand.

Dear Alfred, I think the tube is broken. At least, I check it everyday, my ear conched and ready by the inward bassoon. So it has come to this! I remember the day you ate sardines straight from the tin. Every summer I still make happiness by your mother's recipe.

Encore

Within a month the house
had lost much of its solidity.
Moths clustered, fierce as wrecking balls.
There was no paper anywhere and no sound of composition.

Buoyant

As it happens I am this evening
way hopeful.
A ship, not alone,
rather populated as a small city.
The people walk the deck, which steadies under them.
The ship notices the water
to purr through it.
There are lights in the evening, dances.

I am a walking drum
in the long snout of the ship.
I am under several men on the causeway.
I am dining out on the story.
I am always short of cash.

At the Captain's post, a series
of dots indicate position.
He swings in the chair.
There is a map in him
and a map below him.
If there were music here,
I think he would be singing.

As it happens, I am this evening
ducking under cables.
Ropes connect and unloose.
In the ballroom they are playing
'Daisy My Love'.

In the foreword and the afterword
the ship is all closed up.
In the ocean the citizens
are taking a vote.

In Summer

In summer I sit
and cradle my lip.
The bees ignore me.
Nothing stings me.

III Mother

Autumn Day
—after Rilke

The summer has gone on
past the point of expectation.
In the afternoons now, the ngaio
shades the fish pond.
Soon the first autumn wind
will gust up from the harbour.

It is time for us to gather
the last small peaches;
for the currants to ripen against the fence,
another day or two
pressing sweetness into the fruit.

She who has left us will not come now.
If we see her at all
it will be by chance, among dry leaves,
and she will not know us.

Next Time

The other day my sister was trying to dress you after a spa.
She said you wouldn't lift your leg.
You had your trousers half on.
You said *yes, yes, yes,*
but the foot stayed on the ground.

She thought
this is my mother
there is no way
to make her lift her foot.

My sister laughed when she told me.
She said people were looking at you.

I said, 'Next time make her sit down'.
I said, 'Next time use the family changing room'.
I said, next time get yourself a better mother,
there's something wrong with this one, my sister.
Next time be more careful, this mother is broken, I said.

Great Full Moon, Lowering Behind the Black Hill

The lucky mouth
tastes of strawberries.

★

If searched long enough,
the fruit is found,
hanging or destroyed,
rising or lowering
into the black hills.

★

Softness. Do we love it?
Do we take the long strands
and worship them?
Does it lift us? Do we rise more easily, or is it
like the green vine on the bare peach—
winding, low intent, creeping?

It Was Onward and Upward

It was onward and upward
the wall was green outside and I did not think
I would look at it again.

In the mellow depths of caramel
the day was draining slowly, we were
still walking by the waterside,
the big ship still
sailing in to collect.

If the debt was not a debt
but forgiven
I would go less, I would be
less a curtain pulled across the window.

In medias res the collation, cold and elegant
caught us as we lifted it to our heads
to bite, to swallow.

I will not be back, I said, I came back early.
I'll be leaving I said, taking a seat,
sitting down to bread and salt and a talk with my mother.

If memory serves—but it does not, only
whistles and scratches like a branch against the wall.

If it serves, if it falters, the wall was coloured,
or clear as glass, strained thin by heat and thinking, by the ritual
of a cat, checking the position of fence, washing pile, a leg
known to belong to its owner.

It is Spring, Sometime Late in the Fifties

A girl in a bed under a window,
her skin blossoming red welts, fever rushing.
Her head is hot and heavy, reading strains her eyes.
Through the curtains' gap, japonica bushes,
petals making teacup shapes.

She watches a starling settle in a fork, cock his head.
He hops, leaves, returns. His beak clamps twigs,
rags of wool from the fences, a piece of twine.
A nest among the bone-china flowers.

Sickness laid itself in her,
a speckled egg. Spring is a long brooding,
days pale as her sheet, her companion's eye
bright through the glass. What stirs and rustles in her?
It rises and retreats, like the petals,
abandoning the branches as she tries to count them.

The Lost Coronet

Several times a day former Kings and Queens among men
pass my doorway.
I am almost what they say I am,
a pure receptacle, vacant as crystal.
My bedspread lines itself up in rows of chenille.
Outside the poplar leaves shake:
green silver green.
Lower down a pink flower grows open edgewise
so the centre and the back, thinly veined,
can be seen.

December Letter

If you are able, in the summer daylight,
take your shears and go into the garden.

What License Issued You Away?

Things have changed since you were with us.
We no longer call a spade a spade.

Now we say you are crazy and try to believe it.
Now we say 'she loved us then', and 'there can be no return'.

Connection, light as sunlight through clouds;
as light's flick across valleys, across gorse.

There is no way of saying we are sorry, save to hold you.
There is no way to hold or save you.